Some Chic's Diary
Volume 1

Poems and Short Stories
By
L. Michele

Photography by: Durant Photography

OfficialL.Michele@gmail.com

Formatting, Editing Cover Art, and Graphics by Selina Ahnert of True Beginnings Publishing. Photography by Durant Photography. All Illustrations, Cover Art, and Text are Copyright Protected by: My Original Works. Reference #73391.

Ordering Information:
To order additional copies of this book, please visit Amazon or Createspace at:
https://www.createspace.com/4961447

ISBN-13: 978-0692279939
ISBN-10: 0692279938

Some Chic's Diary
Poems and Short Stories
© L. Michele
First Printing, 2014

Dedication

I dedicate this book to everyone that has believed in me and to everyone who has doubted me; inspirations come in so many forms, it is up to you to use it wisely.

April 11

Well, it's like this.
I don't know what to write about.

My therapist suggested that I start keeping a diary. He felt that I could use this as a tool to release my thoughts, so let me tell you about myself. My name is Myesha Pennington, born from Jackie Foster and Leonard "L.Dogg" Brown. I'm 32 years old, never ever been married, 5 kids, and losing my sanity!

I feel like I'm writing down too much already. Black people don't even go to therapist; that's for crazy people, and I ain't crazy. I just have to do what the hell Child Services tells me to do, to get Kyla and Dawn back.

My oldest, Rashaad, is 18, and I had him when I was 14. I don't know much about his dad. All I know is it was a group of them.

Rashaad got a full scholarship to a big university, but he doesn't contact me much, and my therapist says he might still resent me for living with my Aunt. I couldn't take care of him; I was only 14 and in the damn system, myself! My Mama was in jail for hooking for my raggedy ass daddy, "L.Dogg." It was niggas all over the house at different times of night. My daddy didn't care, as long as he was able to maintain his appetite for jewelry, drugs, and hoes.

Let me go back to my kids. Kiondra is 17, and I met her daddy in a group home. Rashaad was in foster care, until my aunt came for him

when he was 18 months old. Anyway, I thought I was going be with Kiondra's daddy, Dale, but whatever, I hit his ass with back pay, so I will be getting a check for Kiondra 'till she bout 20.

Me and Dale was together for a while, even until we both became legal to not even have to be captive to those terrible homes. Things got bad, and shit got real with me and Dale when I got pregnant with Neal. I just knew Dale was the daddy, bitch my baby came out looking like a damn Mexican! Me and Dale are brown skinned.

I used to work at this fast food place, and this fine ass Mexican named Alfredo used to come through there. He had "black boy swag," he would come speaking Spanish to me, so shit, I asked him for a ride to the bus stop one night, and I offered him some as a tip on the way! That was the dumbest thing ever. Alfredo knew I was pregnant with his baby, but I was in denial. I fought tooth and nail for three years trying to make Dale believe Neal was his baby, and that he looked just like Kiondra. I used to make Alfredo buy the diapers and wipes and tell Dale the Women Center was giving them to me. Dale didn't know who Neal's father was, but he sure knew it wasn't him.

Some of Dale's friends instigated and made him get an at home DNA test! Me being naïve didn't realize why he was being so distant for 6 weeks…. He was waiting on them damn test results. He had them sent to his Mama house.

I'm at home chilling with Kiondra and Neal, and here comes Dale. He called me in the kitchen, like nothing was wrong, but as soon as I stepped foot into the kitchen, I woke up in the emergency room. This bitch almost knocked my head off with a frying pan! He knocked out two of my bottom teeth, a broken nose, and 6 stitches in my chin.

Kiondra had enough sense to dial 911, even though it was her father. So now, here I am, in the emergency room having childhood

flashbacks of child services coming for me, but this time, they were come for my children.

They found our stash of weed, so the kids had to go, and Dale went to jail.

Damn, I ain't think about that night in years.

Well it's getting late; let's try this shit another time.

Im going to get a safe to put this diary in! GN

Myesha Q. Pennington

Choices

A struggle with right and wrong,

A struggle with right from wrong,

Choices, choices are all the things that I have the capability,

to know my responsibility of controlling my destiny.

The past, the past can ride you like a horse,

back down that same course,

Until you come to a fork in the road.

So I struggle with right and wrong,

I struggle with right from wrong.

I close my eyes....

It is my responsibility to have the capability to control MY destiny.

I couldn't stop the leak in the Gulf,

but I can control the words from lips that move without thought....

I opened my eye,

and to my surprise,

I had taken the path of the road to the right.

Is this my future?

Is this where I'm going?

I AM controlling it!

I 'm owning it,

I'm doing it!

Some Chic's Diary

I pass a tree, covered with beautiful fruit,
red and green apples... peaches... pears... and plums.
My journey to destiny has famished me...
AS I lustfully stared at the tree…
choices, choices of what fruit to devour,
knowing THAT I have the capability to make choices accordingly
even with uncertainty
of the probability of this decision not working out for me.
I can't ponder too long,
because there goes opportunity running past me...
I chose the peach;
I closed my eyes and dug my TEETH,
into this sweet and tender beautiful fruit of SPLENDOR.
It felt right,
I'm controlling this,
I'm doing this,
I'm own this with NO influences to ruin this.
I took in every moment of letting the nectar run down my chin,
I closed my eyes what an experience,
and then I realized this peach was the fruit of life.
A life with choices, let me make this peach HISTORY,
for it gave me courage to move forward,
forward to my destiny
even with uncertainty
I'll trust in GOD he will bless me.
Through this journey of life…..
My life.

February 25

Dear Diary,

Normally, I don't even pick up and write this time of night, especially when I get off late from working homicides. I know being a crime scene investigator has its occupational hazards, extreme conditions, and culture shocks! Thank God, I was a Girl Scout, but anyway.

Tonight, while leaving the scene of a burglary, a call went out over the radio advising that shots had been fired in the area. I'm like "aw hell" let me get something to eat, now. I make a U-turn to grab a greasy burger, which happens to be the reason why my hips are spread all over the place, now.

I have to make an appointment in the morning; my cramps have been getting terrible... but anyway.

Dispatch had advised that the subject was last seen heading north bound on Sabor Lane, in a red sedan. So I'm like, great, he is going in the opposite direction. Then dispatch advised that two people had been shot. I immediately grabbed my radio and advised dispatch to show me en route to the scene of the shooting.

You know, I try to do my best and be the best C.S.I. ever.

Anyway, it's cold as hell outside; let me go turn my heater on....

Ok, yeah, so I get to the scene, and its total chaos! I grabbed my camera to photograph my time board. I jumped out of the van and immediately began taking over-all and close up pictures of the scene.

It's better to have too many pictures than not enough. I quickly walked up to the front of the home which is facing the west side of the street. I see paramedics working what appeared to be a black male with multiple gunshot wounds to his upper extremities. I could literally smell his blood.

Now, you know I have seen some shit… unborn babies in toilets, dismembered hands, but I have never arrived on a scene where the victim was actually dying in my face! I squatted down to get better close-up photos of his injuries, and then, our eyes locked.

By habit, I speak to injured victims to keep them calm. I mean, who really wants a camera in their face after they have been seriously injured, right? Hell, I swear it all pays off in court. By the distant stare in his eyes and rattled breathing, I knew his injuries were grave.

I paused for a moment. I felt like I was in the movie *Ghost* when the little black spirit thingy left the body... yeah, I know, totally weird. However, I still prayed for his soul. I don't know about him but I know where I'm going!

The Paramedic hollers, "Hello! Are you coming or staying?"

I'm like, oh shit! At this point my partner, Lydia, arrives at the scene to advise that there are two other scenes to be documented and that she would be en route to the hospital where the victim was being transported by helicopter to Madison Memorial hospital. I proceeded to the other scene located directly to the rear of where the male victim was to discover that the other victim was his mother. So instantly, I'm feeling like crap, because I know her son is about to die.

She was grazed throughout her body with a high powered assault rifle. In the midst of paramedics trying to treat her, all you could hear was her cry was, "Where is my Son? Where is my baby?"

My heart melted. I mean, I am a parent, and I couldn't fathom her confusion. I wiggled my way through the melee to take photographs of her injuries, and when I leaned in, she grabbed my coat and asked me how was her son doing.

Shit… I was stuttering like a stick shift car with no gas, so I told her a detective would be with her, shortly. I felt like the biggest liar! A detective was going to talk to her, but I knew her son probably passed before being air lifted to safety.

I stepped outside of the house to follow paramedics as they whisked her away. My Sgt. approaches me to give me a rundown of what allegedly occurred, and that her son did pass away. The son basically was tired of the mother's boyfriend beating up on her every time he got drunk. When the son confronted the boyfriend, obviously all fuckin' hell broke loose. It is terribly unfortunate it had to end that way for them.

I am struggling with erasing the images that I saw tonight; I mean, that young man didn't even have a chance trying to protect his mother.

I'm glad to be in my cozy wozy bed. It was cold as hell out there; 39 degrees in Florida is bullshit. My nose was running, and there is dried up snot on my collar and sleeve. I decided, long ago, that I could not be a doctor or a nurse, because I don't feel I am mentally equipped to deal with the sick and dying… ironically, I can deal with the dead. Your body is just a vessel where your soul once was, and where it goes afterwards is up to you.

I have been doing Crime Scene for quite some time, now. I personally love it; my ex-husband can't stand it. I suppose that is why he is an ex-husband. The hours are very demanding, sometimes, but he never complained about the gifts. I'd rather masturbate than sleep with him, anyway. Perhaps that is another reason why he is an ex-husband.

I did meet this attorney; she is a real fox. I see her every time I have depositions at the City Building.

Relationships are for people in black and white movies. Jeff and I were married for seven years, before I found out he was screwing around with that basketball-mom, Lu-Anne. I told them other mothers I ain't like her, coming round practice with them tight ass t-shirts, nipples always looking erect! LOL Just not basketball-mom appropriate.

Well anyway, I'm hitting the sack.

Sara

June 8

Hey Sassy Diary Lady,

I am so glad finals are over! Math is for morons... I'm ready to get drunk. I think tomorrow I'm going to invite Evelyn and those other hoes over.

Last time we got drunk, the mean old man down stairs called security! Evelyn opens the door, and pot smoke is billowing out the door like a Snoop video, or some shit. Thank God my Dad owns the building; I'd be like so jailed, or something. LMAO! I swear I wasn't smoking, though. I study too much! No time for burning out!

Anyway, I went into Sinsex and bought this vibrator the size of, like I don't know, like some guy I'VE NEVER been with! LOL! I don't know what the hell possessed me to get it; I'm just tired of these girls always having some freak-fest story to talk about. Cucumbers, condoms, LUBRICANTS! I feel badly that I have never had an orgasm from anal sex or squirted water fountain style while having an orgasm. I need to step out of my sexual box.

This sounds strange, LOL, I picked a movie Funky Cooch Lovin'.... lol I already know it sounds gross. Nobody really loves a Funky Cooch... but I'm visual, so the pictures on the cover were interesting! LOL! I'm laughing at my sexuality that is undiscovered.... to be found by a battery-operated lover!

And, I'm a fake rapper. I'm so lame. I'm so glad this is my diary and no one else's. I think I am going to have a nice, hot bubble bath, tonight, and experiment with this thing. Wait, let me read it again... it is called "Man Handle".....LMAO!

I think I'm going to get Man Handled, tonight!

I should pull a keg of beer next to the tub with a long funnel straw!!!!! AND GET MAN HANDLED!! I am beyond crazy. It's almost funny enough to update my status with: Well, let me go do my thing. LOL if I get "man handled" tonight, I'll let you know!!!!!!!!!!!!!!!!!!!!!!!!!!!!!!!

Trish

"He was younger than me" PT I.

And he was younger than me,
but nowhere near as wise as me,
but no one could grab my thighs like he,
and he was younger than me.

"Age ain't nothing but a number,
going down is gonna be your thang."
I know you're full of energy,
but do you really think you can hang,
and he is younger than me.

Come sit on Mama Lap, I'll be your Sugar Mama,
getting stamps on your passport to go to the Bahamas,
pack light no need for pajamas, don't worry, sweet heart.
I'll talk to your Mama, because you are younger than me….

All wet behind the ears, breathe smelling like Similac.
I love when you choke me and fuck me from the back,
You smiling and blushin, because I taught you that.
You never heard a kitty purr like dat:
It's because I ain't a Kitty bitch,
I'm a cougar, slidin' up on ya to school ya,
You think I love you, but I fooled ya.
I mean, because you are younger than me.

My juices run down your cock like wine grapes in a vineyard,
fermented to the second on the clock,
you like the way this pussy pop
and the sounds I make when I climb on top.
Mmmh yes, can you feel this pussy get hot...
You like it; can you take the way I grind my hips...
on your lips.... and he was younger than me.

I saw you with your girlfriend the other day.
Does she know how to put that whole dick away...
I mean, like swallow it and gargle it,
spit it out and suck it back up or rub it on her face?
Does she sit on it and bounce up and down
like a cloud FULL of precipitation...
Love come down...ooh, you make
My Love Come Down....
Probably not... because, SHE IS younger than me.

At the end of the training day, I put you away,
when it is time for NO work and no play,
because I need HE who is older than ME.
Fuck my mind just like my BODY.
After all, YOU are younger than me.

Dear Journal,

As you know, Sean and I have been engaged for 2, almost three years. Well, I think we may be growing apart. He asked me had I ever thought about having a threesome.

What kind of question is that?

I was completely under the impression that our sex was magical on its own! So, I voiced my opinion to him, and he seemed understanding to it but very persistent. I don't know how I feel about that.

I thought that if you loved somebody, you didn't share them, right? I mean, I know there are different strokes for different folks, but I am not sure I want Sean stroking different folks! Sean feels because I have been with a woman before, that I should indulge in this with him. I have never had a lesbian relationship before, just a few shots of tequila. Random shit happens to random people!

He didn't stress the issue after I told him hell no and where to go find the extension cord to go blow up the air mattress in the living room. We were cool, after that. I know his mind is all over the place now because mines certainly is. I am not insecure about another woman performing better than me, but I just feel like no matter who you are what you do, some men can't keep themselves to themselves.

We had this conversation the other night, and this evening he brings it up, again. He and I have discussed a lot of things and have established a great amount of trust, but I have not had the best past relationships, as far as it pertains to monogamy. I don't know how I really feel. A part of me wants to say yes, and the other half probably the better half of me wants to say hell no... Hell fuck no!! A friend of mines, Wendy, told me how she and her husband were into "swinging" and everything was all fine and dandy until she came home early to try and surprise this negro with dinner for his new promotion to find him with their usual dessert Kama Sutra'ing it up in the living room.... LOL... Can you say awkward screwed up moment.

I hated him for doing that to her. I suppose those are the CONS of having an open marriage or relationship. So, I just remain cordial when I see them. As for Sean and his genius ideas about bringing another woman into the bedroom is leading me to believe that he is cheating on me. I haven't found anything, and yes, I do snoop through his personal belongings and I can't find Jack! LOL! I tell you what was funny, I was going through his phone, one night, to find a picture of a smoothly waxed chocolate twat, and boy was I upset until I realized it was mines!!! LOL #teamfatcrotch.

I wouldn't mind sliding up on another player on team fat crotch. I just really don't believe I would be able to trust him, after that, especially if I let Wendy get in my ear. I hear him coming in, now. Let me go so I can hook my man up proper! Good night.

Rachel <------ #teamfatcrotch

Thinking

I was thinking about you today, did you feel it? I thought you felt the goose bumps rise on your arms at the thought my touch. I thought I saw the hair rise on the back of your neck as if an Angel whispered inspiration in your ear.

I was thinking about you today. You sure you didn't feel the erection you had when you vaguely smelled my perfume on your pillow? I thought you felt the fluttering of butterfly wings gently against the lining of your stomach, when you got lost in the moment of bliss of how sweetly I kissed your lips.

Did you think about me today, like did you think about how warm our bodies are when we lay next to each other? Or how moist the sheets are after we have showed each other? How much we have missed each other by thinking about one another....

I thought about you today. I thought about how excited you get when I hug you tightly and wrap my legs around your waist and how I can feel your bulge in my sweet place.

I thought about you today. I thought about what I was going to make you for dinner when you came home and how I would set the table with two candles and crank up some jazz sounds to drown the other music we will make on top of the table I set with two candles...

You thought I was coming until you stopped and pulled it out and let all my juices fill your mouth...

You thought you were done, until I grabbed and pulled you closer to me. I felt you grow, again…

You thought you were done when you felt my legs tremble like an N.Y. earthquake aftershock…

You thought you were done when I turned over to catch my breath, and whispered…. I think I want to do it, again… ya think? ;)

A Friend, a pillow, and a lap

In desperate need of a friend, a pillow, and a lap.

My heart is broken, and the crack has allowed my soul to escape and is desperately roaming the earth for its mate.

When love feels good, it is the most blessed feeling that God has created the nervous system for, and when it hurts, it's like 1000lbs of air squeezing at my lifeless lungs crushing my empty belly twisting my spine and paralyzing my limbs.

My breathing is labored, and the tears burn my skin like acid. My body is flaccid, I'm trembling and shaking, and my heart is aching.

Please, rub my back and comfort me; please, hug my soul and console me. I just need a friend, a pillow, and a lap.

When I close my eyes, it's like all I can see are the memories that used to be real. Or were they real? I miss the person I thought you were... Does that make me delusional... Does that make you a fake... Don't taint what is pure, for my love for you is without sin... Not yet corrupted by deception of selfish lies... selfish enough to disregard tears from Un-TAINTED....... love…

Was I the one that you wanted to feel during sex? I wonder, I ask, I cry, all I need is a friend, a pillow, and a lap.

What made her better than me?

Perhaps, it was my inequities of my baggage that I have acquired from endless, meaningless relationships.

I don't want advice, and the questions I ask are rhetorical. I really

just need a friend, a pillow, and a lap. I share with you because I care to; it's not a dare to; expose myself or be allowed to indulge yourself as my friend with a pillow and a lap, and possibly an ambient.

June 9

Ok Diary listen,

So, I man handled myself, last night. I am totally embarrassed, because I can't believe I have been missing out on pleasuring myself to study.

Well first of all, let me tell you, last night I drew myself a bath around 10 p.m. I didn't get out of the tub until like a quarter to 1 a.m. LOL! I decided, maybe, I needed to set the mood. I lit a gazillion scented candles and dropped a few scented rose petals in the warm water. I slipped into the tub and forgot the damn toy, so needless to say, I jumped out of the tub to go get it and slipped across the tile floor running back! LOL! What a kill joy is that? I'm so glad the water was really hot. So hot that when I slid back into the tub, the hot water scorched my ass. I hate that, and then, it itched… well, whatever.

So now, I'm in the tub with this Man Handler that is bigger than anybody I have been with. I turn the thing on, and the tub becomes like a whirl pool! So, I start going to town. I almost drowned! No kidding, because the orgasms that I had were like none I have ever experienced! I guess I was man handled; I had become bamboozled into constant masturbation.

Getting man handled is definitely something that I wanted to share. So, I kind of got carried away and called Evelyn over. Let me describe Evelyn to you. She is like super fine. I'd give her like a 23 inch waist, and then, other inches spread out how they should be. Ass for days, oh my!

So whatever, I call her she picks and is like, "Hey Chic what's poppin?" My randomly perverted self says, "This Pussy." It was a definite awkward moment, because... its EVELYN. She's super gorgeous, and this would make for that one story I have to tell after college. It's like a silent rule that goes with the part about words unspoken.

Anyway, she lives on the 19th floor, so I know she will be right up. I felt a certain emotion as if this was supposed to happen. I threw the phone on the floor, blinked back into lust, and I looked up, and Evelyn was there like a ghost. Good thing the water was still warm. She smiled at me and told me that we had company; I'm thinking, wow, I like this math problem.

In the shadow of the gazillion candles that are lit, a cross between Jesus and Idris Alba comes strolling in the bathroom, literally swinging his dick in his hand. I grabbed Evelyn and was like, "Girl, I don't know what the hell you got going on, but this is not regular shit." She replies with, "I felt bad for your lil horny ass. I saw that Sinsex bag in your closet yesterday." She whispered in my ear and gently slid her naked body into my giant size tub.

Yes, I'm a brat, even Mandingo can fit in here!

As she slid into the tub, she used her legs like octopus arms and wrapped them around my waist. The nice chocolate brother standing there grabbed Evelyn's ponytail and pulled her head back, only so shove all of his mankind into her mouth. I found myself gently caressing her nipples with my tongue, in small circular motions. I have done this, before. I just did it the way I would like to feel.

He sweetly let out gentle moans. Didn't expect gentle sounds from this giant, because he stood at least 6'4, so his big ass was kneeling on the side of the tub while Evelyn literally man handled him!

She stopped a moment and starred at me. She twisted me around, thrusting me over the other side of the tub. She spread my suds soaked butt cheeks as if she lost something. I was nervous but went along with everything. She used her tongue to meet the crevices where suds had fallen. As she pleasured me, chocolate dream stepped into the tub and got to stroking her from the back.

So, the first thing going through my mind is, "Who is this dude? They're so raw dogging it, I've got magnums and other stuff in my vanity drawer". At any rate, the stroking had to have been getting good to her, because her tongue searching endlessly inside of me was becoming more intense. With her face still buried in the back of me, she grabbed my perky "C" cups and squeezed as if I were going to express milk.

I then began to feel weak; I could tell that the both of them did, too. We three were about to reach harmony! He pulled his bulging counterpart out of Evelyn and squirted what I would believe to be hot babies on her back. He belted out the sexiest man grunt I've ever heard, but then again, I purchased a dildo that is bigger than any guy I have been with! LOL. I am such a nerd!

Anyway, Fuck yeah, we did. It was really nice. So since then, I have used the thing like 6 times already. I am trying to see if I can get the same effect as that first orgasm. Not really what I thought. Well, Evelyn and I can keep a secret; I can tell her I have masturbated 6 more times since they left. Yeah, but the guy come to find out they have been dating for like 9 months. He was the surprise that she had been talking about.

What the hell, Evy! What a way to introduce your best friend to your MAN!! Oh, and I didn't know that the movie I brought was a double feature. I think I am going to pass on "Black Love Butt Pluggin'"

Well anyway, I'm tired. I cried with the last two orgasms I had.

Trish,

p.s. I need more C batteries

Some Chic's Diary

The next paragraph that you are about to read, depicts a paragraph from your diary if you were into voyeurism. Complete this journal entry with your fantasy.

Voy-eur

1: one obtaining sexual gratification from observing unsuspecting individuals who are partly undressed, naked, or engaged in sexual acts; *broadly* **:** one who habitually seeks sexual stimulation by visual means

I watched you walk across the street to the fresh market. You laughed at a small child walking a dog. I didn't realize how arousing watching you was. I felt like a stalker watching you from my balcony... but nothing was more thrilling than peeling my satin robe off of my shoulders and slowly stroking my nipples... Your oblivion to a stranger watching made my love tongue rattle like an angry snake... I slipped my fingers down between my legs and closed my eyes. The vision of you rinsing soapy suds from your body after the gym is past arousing. You have no clue of the view that I have from apartment balcony into your apartment... or do you?

_____

_____

_____

_____

_____

_____

_____

_____

_____

_____
_____
_____
_____
_____
_____
_____
_____
_____
_____
_____
_____
_____
_____
_____
_____
_____
_____
_____

Love yourself

"Don't wake me"

His presence makes caterpillars develop
into their next stage of life….

His skin is so chocolaty,
he makes me want to bite him,
and lick him,
I'm trying to consume all of him with one swallow,
pounding my insides like I'm hollow…

I feel him in me like his organ belongs in me.
It fits so perfectly,
my chocolate dream, please don't wake me…

L. Michele

"All Eyes on He"

All Eyes on He,
I was smitten by the way his jeans fit,
he walks like he has big dick….
All Eyes On He,
His pheromones pumped passion,
his swag sways around him
like bees around a honey comb,
he can taste my honey comb,
he can have my honey comb…
All Eyes on He…

April 9

Dear Diary,

I have never felt this way about a man before!

I mean I have had my fair share of men. Like Steven the elevator repair man, or Josh the mechanic. Anyway, it is just really something about Ryan.

I knew from the first time I laid eyes on him, we would have the most sexually explicit session of love making known to mankind. So, I was very forward and sent him those little edible flowers. I figured he like fruits and stuff.

Jillian, his secretary, told him that it came from me. I tried to keep it a secret, but I think she was a little disturbed about walking in on me shoving "ben wah" balls between by legs right before a meeting. I mean gosh, what the hell she thinks the damn phone system is for.

He sent me an instant message asking me to dinner, tonight. Of course, I accepted. I went over to Meagan Boutique to see if I could find something sexy. I found this sexy purple and black slip dress. I have my sexy lace bra and panty set I have been dying to show some lady's son.

Well, let me hurry up and take a shower. I have to shave my legs and slap some hair remover on this here twat. I didn't have time to make it to the waxing salon. Well, it still gives the same effect, no hair just straight smooth cat. I'm almost certain the way Ryan carries himself, he likes a bald twat.

I want to masturbate before he gets here, it takes the edge off. Anyway, let me get ready. Hopefully, I have something exciting to talk about, tomorrow.

Mandy

"Imagine That"

The way it feels when he pushes himself inside of me…
Flesh to flesh, it grows, I quiver he thrust deeper…
He was searching for my soul, I thrust back,
he challenged my pelvic cavity...
With my left foot upon his right peck
and my right leg over his left shoulder,
gently, yes gently worked me over,
Imagine that…

"To Be"

I just want to be…
I want to be his epitome of love and loyalty.
I want to be his epitome of orgasms and fantasy.
I just want to be…
I want to smell his skin on mine.
I want to be what he sees when he reads between the lines.
I want to be his eternity, just forever loving me.
If he asked me to Wed thee, I'd say yes...

"While he was in me"

While he was in me, all I saw was your face...
He stroked my body at a different pace.
The salt of his skin had a different taste.
While he was in me, all I saw was your face...
I wanted to taste you, I wanted to feel you,
and all I wanted was you.
But your selfish, muted demons chased you away from me…

"Consistent"

The sound of raindrops on the pavement is consistent like our love
It never skips a beat, can I sleep here?
With my head on your chest?
I want to hear your heartbeat,
its consistent and loyal to you like my love;
it never skips a beat,
my favorite monotonous sound...

April 10

Dear Diary,

Well it happened....

Let me begin with when he picked me up. He had several long-stemmed purple roses. My panties got wet instantly; purple is my favorite color. He smelled so sexy that when he hugged me, if I had a dick, it would've poked him. To my surprise, he was trying to remain gentlemanly when I gently kissed his neck while we hugged each other. I hope the neck kiss wasn't doing too much for a first date.

So, we get to the restaurant, and I give him the liberty of ordering dinner for me. I mean, he has got to have good taste, especially if he plans on eating my pussy, later. He ordered lobster Alfred.

We have a lot more in common than what I expected. He has a 14 year old daughter that lives with his ex-wife. I have no children or ex-wife! Thank God! LOL! He enjoys poetry, working out, and antique cars.

After we finished dinner, he wanted to show me a gazebo that was on the east side, overlooking one of the most beautiful lakes in the city. It's clean and has live animals that have escaped being born with multiple body parts at birth. I was a little nervous, at first, because I really like him. I already felt a little goofy when he carried me on his back to the gazebo, because the grass was a little damp. It was playful, but I know he felt my warm twat on his back.

L. Michele

He gently let me down on the steps of the gazebo, and without warning, he lifted me onto the wooden railing. I was a little nervous, because he pushed himself between my legs, and I felt his Kielbasa! He pushed his face close to mines, and I could smell the fermented red wine on his breath. He kissed me long and deep, just like how I like to be stroked. He picked me up, forcing me to straddle my legs around his waist.

Automatically, porn music starts playing in my head, but the soft porn kind of music, an acoustic guitar and a harp….. okay, anyway. He gently lays me on my back on the bench, which looked like it was made for this kind of impromptu shit. He reached in his back pocket (that dirty devil) and pulls out the condom, built for men hung like horse. While kissing me and holding me steady, he managed to put the condom on with one hand. The wind was blowing and the sweet smell of gardenias took over the night air. He put his entire man hood into my woman hood and made me sing like a lost Polynesian bird.

Whatever sense that makes, nothing with wings should get lost. He pulled it out and shoved his face down there as if he were bobbing for damn apples! Needless to say, it has been a while, so while I was climaxing from that awesome tongue action, he stops and pushed his rod back into me. I'm like, "Gosh damn, Ryan, I should've sent you that fruit basket long ago."

We both came, together. He grabbed me so tightly and sweetly, I forgot we were in a gazebo, in public. We nervously giggled and got our clothing together. He piggy backed me to the car. I slid off of his back, and he spun me around like a pretty little ballerina, then he kissed me……. AAAAAHHHHHH!

Does this make me a hoe? LOL! I mean, I think we hit it off pretty well. AAAAAHHHHHH!!

Some Chic's Diary

Look, he just text me, "Had a great time. Maybe, we can get together this weekend for a movie or something, and you taste delicious!" AAAAAAAHHHH! Okay, does this still make me a hoe?? I'm going to bed! I can't wait until this weekend.

Mandy

My Confession

Yes, I have a confession...

I am a HOE, and I know it...

Just one will do fits perfectly...

If it's too big, it won't do, and if it's too small, then HELL NAW.

Cost me a lot, sometimes, but I get it when I can get it.

Even when the bills are due, that sinful nature comes over me.

I got one similar to this 6.5 inch, already, but it's too pointy...

That shit hurts, to make me feel sexier, it's almost always worth it, you just gotta know how to work it!

Shit, lemme tell you my Gator pumps by Guess, really go with everything, but these red suede pumps over here really get me going...

What?

What did you think I was talkin' bout?

YOU just nasty, but I have a confession, I am a HOE, a SHOE HOE, that is!!

Just Like This

Well, then it should go just like this.
Take me over there, you know, where you are bliss.
That's it, suckle on my left tit
then stroke my clit…

Yep, actually, it should go like this...

Take me into your soul,
love me, make me whole, delve into my spirit lining.
Look, your love is so blinding,
it keeps me shining
when I think about us grinding.

Yep, it should feel like that.

Lie me on my back,
push my legs back just like that,
take it from me, Daddee, I won't fight back,
watch how I twist and turn and arch my back….

Uhm that's right just like that!

L. Michele

Can you feel me grabbing you, gripping, and thrusting?
Oh GOD, I think I'm busting...
Everything is flowing from me;
this is where and how I want to be.
Let's explore, Daddee,
give me more,
No, my legs ain't sore.
Didn't you hear me? Give me more!
Love me, Hug me, lick me,
hold me down, and just become me.
Yes hunnee, cum in me.
Fill up my cup till it runneth over....
Bite my neck and then my shoulder,
Hold me tight and bend me over.
They don't make 'em like me, you gotta mold her.
She's a Taurean lover
that knows how to please her Sagittarius lover.
He's badder than a mother.....
hush my mouth, put it in my mouth.
Let's switch positions, so we can go down south.

We both cum; the moans we make roar like thunder.
Can the neighbors hear us is what I wonder?
Turn me over, lie me on my belly,
Yes, I feel it in my belly
ride me and make me scream WHOA NELLY!

Some Chic's Diary

I feel all of you consume all of me
no longer two but one entity.
You lick my lobe and whisper gently,
"Is this where and how you want to be,
tell me sweetie can you feel me deeper and deeper inside of you,
tossing and turning you don't know what to do,
bit your lips and twist your face,
slow down baby and cum at my pace."

Again, we climb to ecstasy, erupting like a dormant volcano,
trembling and shaking, I'm out of breath,
this erotic feeling that Shakespeare claims is near death.
We turn over with love's hangover.
I place my head on your chest,
this is the part I love the best.
As you run your fingers through my hair,
I begin to stare into thin air.
Your heart beat is with mines,
no longer a pair.
You took me there…
over there… with you in bliss,
and that's how it is.
It really happens JUST LIKE THIS!!!!

"Just Like This, Again..."

He blew my back out like a used tire on a desolate road.
He stroked me softly like petals from a rose;
it felt good to him…
The way he gripped my hips, it showed...
The way he leaned in it and made my toes curl,
he knew it felt good to me
By the way I tugged at the sheets
and gritted my teeth.
He pulled my hair as he spanked my derriere.
Remember how it happened in Just like this.
Well, he took me over there;
Over there to bliss...

Untitled

How awkward is it, not knowing if what is about to happen is wrong. It's only hard to determine, because it has happened for so long.

"Make sure everybody is asleep," he whispered in a tone I dare not defeat.

His over-sized hands touched my adolescent body. Didn't feel good or bad; him touching my body was a torture of a memory to have.

"Turn over, let me put it in your butt."

"No, that's nasty!" I whispered with fear. If you were a fly on the wall, not a nice conversation to hear from a girl with 6 whole years of experience in life.

From 6-7 till I was at least 11, he did things to me only women his age would be obliged to spread their thighs, breathing and panting with sweet moans and cries.

Don't make me say I love you, for I am a child. This SHIT IS WILD, FOR I AM ONLY A CHILD.

This only happened on summer nights when he came to visit.

"Taste it, rub it on your lips, it's not pee, trust me…" were the words he would breathe when he'd cum on me. He would rub himself against my panties decorated with lace, filled with uncertain feeling; I'd cover my face… Please. take me from this place…

For I had no breast or curves. but HE still had the nerve to continue to touch me like a perv… by the time I got old enough to realize these summer nights were wrong, it almost seemed expected. My feelings were affected, because my sexuality had been tested way before time suggested.

Yes, it stopped. It eventually ceased. It's weird as an adult now to see him in the streets. He is grown with a daughter now; SHE is as beautiful and tender as I was...

Oh GOD, help him. I wonder if he prays and asks God to forgive him and to protect his baby girl from men like him... Can you see those visions from back then...but wait, he must pray for the men in his family, first, the only way to break the generational curse? Curse not sent from forefather but sometimes our fathers that turn cheeks to pain caused in the heart of mothers, because the inconvenience of their baby has been jaded by the perverse spirits that have attached to the perverse minds with the perverse lines that are being whispered... Into my ear...

How do I battle these demons that have left visible lesions of scars? Scars that have destroyed my chances of trusting a man, knowing the difference between loving and lusting for a man, knowing the difference between saving myself for myself, and saving myself from myself. Do his demons rest upon his shoulders, or do they rest their head on his chest? Can they hear the blood pumping through his veins and interpret where it should build up... in his penis... or in his brain giving him a massive headache that goes nowhere... like the memories you have embedded in my mind, like the first taste of cotton candy and cookies & cream ice cream.

My first kiss was from you, my first touch was from you, does it feel the same from every man, or is this touch of similarities of grandfathers, uncles, cousins or family friends. I am confused how to let a man love me, they have only hurt me, and pushed themselves on me, and always seemed to be related to me.

I'll never tell, I could never tell, the truth would bring about a living hell. Father again, please, protect me; please, protect HER, I pray in the name of Jesus to remove this generational curse.

Acknowledgements

I would like to thank Jesus Christ as my Savior, because he is my homeboy. He knows how to take you to the edge and bring you back. This book was inspired by a gumbo of real life inspiration, people, places, and things. Some people were realer than other; some places were better than others. Aside from reality, imagination has evoked a combination of relatable experiences for me to share with you.

I will also give a special thank you to the original team "Thinkers" you know who you are! I hope that the same inspiration that I have received from others through their literature can be reciprocated through mine!

About The Author

L. Michele, a Miami Florida native, has been writing for over 20 years. She received her first copyright in 1996 for a series of Children's Stories that she had won several literary awards for in Middle School and High School. Upon completing High School and giving birth to her son, she went on to college to become a Crime Scene Investigator. She worked for different law enforcement agencies in the Miami area, until she decided to pursue her passion for writing and poetry, which was inspired by her many experiences in the crime scene investigation field.

L.Michele is also a host of an open mic poetry venue, *Majestical Lips,* located in the Miami design district. She has been sharing her passion of poetry and entertaining with Majestical Lips since 2012.

In May of 2013, L.Michele released her first poetry album entitled *Some Chic's Poetry,* which is available on ITunes, Amazon, and

Google Play. This album allows you to hear her sultry voice as she recites "He Was Younger Than Me" and "The Way I Feel About Chocolate."

You can look forward to a sophomore poetry album and Volume 2 of *Some Chic's Diary* in the upcoming months.

To stay abreast of L.Michele's events and new projects, you can follow her on:

Twitter - @LMichele2

Facebook - www.facebook.com/AuthorL.Michele

Instagram - @Lau_Mii